ONLY GOD KNOWS…
WHY!!!
God's Lovely Butterfly
Darlene Kearney

Darlene Kearney

ONLY GOD KNOWS... WHY!!!

God's Lovely Butterfly

Darlene Kearney

Pearly Gates Publishing LLC
INSPIRING CHRISTIAN AUTHORS TO BE AUTHORS

Pearly Gates Publishing, LLC, Houston, Texas (USA)

Only God Knows…Why!!!

ONLY GOD KNOWS…WHY!!!
God's Lovely Butterfly

Amazon Assigned ISBN 13: 9798556612761
Independently Published

For information and bulk ordering, contact:
Pearly Gates Publishing, LLC
Angela Edwards, CEO
P.O. Box 62287
Houston, TX 77205
BestSeller@PearlyGatesPublishing.com

Darlene Kearney

What Others Are Saying...

"Wow!"

"Darlene went through so much."

"Darlene loves God."

"Darlene is so strong!"

"Darlene is a go-getter!"

"Darlene loves taking care of the community."

"Darlene wears many hats."

Dedication

This book is first dedicated to
GOD,
the Head of my life, my Father, and my
EVERYTHING.

This book is also dedicated to
my two younger children, who have been the reason I have
not given up…my **WHY:**
Joseph and Serenity.
You both push me daily to go harder and
to give you the life I never had.

Darlene Kearney

Acknowledgments

Special recognition and appreciation are given to the following because they have motivated me to be the best person I can be:

My dear Mother, who made me the person I am today: strong and fearless.

The love of my life, Keith.

My best friend, Doris, who has been my cheerleader, a shoulder to cry on, a listening ear, and for just being there when I was going through the lowest times in my life.

My godsister, Athena, for always remaining the same and loving me, believing in me, and telling me how much she is proud of me.

My favorite cousin and guardian angel, Greg.

My beloved angel and sister-in-law, Angie, who has listened to my cries, laughter, and witnessed my ups and downs.

My newest angel, Twynette, who I have never seen in person. We met on Facebook several years ago, and she encouraged me to keep going, no matter how many trials and tribulations I faced.

My hairstylists, Drea and Taz.

My true friends who have been there, my "play sisters" who have turned into my family, and my godchildren who make me feel special.

Rosie for being such an inspiration to me, pushing me, and believing in me.

My church family at Gateway Community Church.

My former coworkers at Harris County Jail and YMAC Harris County.

My work staff at L-H Transitional Center.

My clients of Faith & Favor Multi-Services and God's Lovely Butterflies Maternity Home.

Through the good, the bad, and the storms of life, each of you has strengthened me on this journey. I love you all.

Preface

This book was written to encourage all women of the world to push through and to also speak to the men to have a better outlook on women.

I have been through so many things in life that would have caused the average person to throw in the towel. When I was younger, I used to cry myself to sleep at night. I felt I was not good enough. I felt unloved. I believed I was the black sheep of the family.

In 2010, God gave me a vision. Throughout the years, that vision began to be pieced together. I then discovered I am God's Lovely Butterfly—no matter how others mistreat, hurt, or harm me. He prepared me for everything I prayed for.

After all, how can I help other women if I had not gone through "it" myself?

Introduction

On the pages of this book, you will learn how Darlene turned her childhood pain into adult purpose. No matter what the enemy threw her way, she never gave up. She speaks of God's favor, despite the treacherous journey and choices made along the way. Her past does not define her.

When life threw her curve balls, Darlene refused to grow bitter. Despite her brokenness, she got up every day and provided for her family. From the time of her birth, she attests to numerous times God spared her life for such a time as this.

As a takeaway, Darlene would like you to know that no matter what goes on in your life, *"Do **NOT** give up!"* Good things happen when you do not give up or give in.

Darlene Kearney

Table of Contents

Chapter One

I Thank God

I wonder: Can anyone else endure all I have and still be in their right mind? It seems my life has been a book in the making since the day I was born. As I reflect on my life, I realize I am a survivor who made it through without allowing bitterness to take hold of my heart.

I thank God for the peace of mind He gave me. I am here, not in the grave due to suicide.

I thank God for the strength He gave to not turn to drugs or alcohol amid my trials.

Most of all, I thank God I do not look like what I have been through.

Along the way, I have had to forgive so many people who hurt me. What a long journey it has been, as I gained more and more strength to fight another day. Today, I can testify and attest to the fact that God has me here for a reason. I am so grateful for my children…my **WHY**…my motivation.

At first, when things started to happen in my life, I thought and felt like God did not love me. I was angry at Him and questioned, *"GOD, WHY ME?"*

He gently whispered, *"Why **NOT** you? I love you. You are My anointed one. I trust you and will never put more on you than you can bear."*

I recall at that moment, I cried my eyes out and began to think about all the things God brought me through. I shouted, *"Thank You, Jesus! Use me, Lord, to be Your messenger, to help other women heal through hurt, betrayal, lies, deceit, pain, sorrow, single motherhood…"* and the list goes on and on.

I have experienced parent hurt, family hurt, children hurt, friend hurt, job hurt, church hurt, and relationship hurt…**BUT GOD!** I learned to pray and cry my way through each instance, keeping myself busy to hide my pain.

Amidst it all, I have been blessed to wear many hats:

- Mother
- Godmother
- Sister
- Friend
- Aunt
- Daughter
- Certified Nurse Assistant
- Medical Assistant
- Certified Community Health Worker
- Co-Author
- Author
- Certified Life Coach
- HIV/AIDS Trainer
- Licensed Chemical Dependency Intern
- Recovery Coach

- ❖ Officiate
- ❖ Notary
- ❖ Proud Business Owner of God's Lovely Butterflies Maternity Home, Faith & Favor Multi-Services, and My Promise to You Officiate Services

And so, my story begins. **I thank God** I am here to tell it.

Chapter Two

Challenged Since the Womb

I was born in 1979. It was a time when prenatal care was not as advanced as it is today, which was part of the reason my mother did not know she was pregnant with twins. I suppose that lack of knowledge was partly attributed to my twin sister consuming the majority of food and nutrients needed for my survival in the world.

I exited my mother's womb at a whopping **two pounds.**

Due to my low birth weight, I had to remain in the hospital to gain more weight. My twin went home with my mother. While in the hospital, I received a severe burn on my left leg from the incubator—something the hospital never told my mother about. She learned about my injury weeks later when she came to visit me. Yes, **weeks** later. My mother had to care for my twin at home, making it difficult for her to go to the hospital to care for me. You might be surprised to learn my mother did not file charges against the hospital. Her reason? She said, *"We didn't believe in doing that."* It was a different time…a different age. I am grateful to God that I survived. To this day, the scar on my thigh still bothers me from time to time.

Where was my father, you might be wondering? Throughout the years, I never saw him. Later in my life, I learned he was married and that his wife refused to accept my sister and me. As a result, my mother raised us without any help or support from him.

I know raising twins alone had to be difficult for my mother, but she managed to do it. Not only did she manage, but she was also remarkably successful at it! Was my mother perfect? No. What person on this earth is? Whether a product of circumstance or her own upbringing, she was strict and meant business. Regardless of whatever she was going through, not a day went by when we did not have clean clothes and a home-cooked meal. For the entirety of my childhood, we lived in government-subsidized apartments. My mother never had a full-time job, choosing instead to babysit and take children back and forth to school.

Chapter Three

Why in the World Did I Lie?

1989 is a year I will never forget. It was the worst year of my life — the one when my mother mercilessly beat me for telling a lie. I clearly recall the pain and blood. If only I had told the truth, I would not have gotten beaten that way.

Let me take you back with me to that moment…

While using the bathroom, I realized there was not enough toilet tissue on the roll. I quickly got up to grab a new roll out of the closet, which, I am sad to say, was blocked by a bottle of red iodine. I thought the iodine was closed tightly, but it was not. It fell to the floor and immediately began spilling its contents onto the floor. As I eyeballed the disaster, I did my best to hurriedly clean it up before my mother found out what I had done. I was not quick enough.

My mother walked in, saw the red mess all over the floor, and asked, *"What happened? What is this on the floor?"*

"My nose was bleeding." That was the first thing that popped into my mind and out of my mouth. I prayed she would accept my lie, but I knew she did not believe one word by the look on her face.

"Don't lie to me!" she said. (I told you she means business.)

I started crying. I knew I was in big trouble for both spilling the iodine **AND** lying.

As my mother started cleaning up the spill, I cleaned myself up and then went into the living room. Shortly after getting settled, I was approached by her—wooden broom in hand.

"Why did you lie?" she screamed. She beat me with that broom for what felt like hours.

Afterward, I was bloody from head to toe and in excruciating pain. I cried out to God, *"What did I do to deserve being beat like **THAT**?!"*

The next day, it was as if the beating never happened. My mother prepared my sister and me for school as usual. Barely two words were spoken when she dropped us off. When I walked into the classroom, my bruised and battered appearance immediately caught my teacher's eye.

"Come here, Darlene," she gently beckoned. When she asked me what happened, what did I do? I lied.

"I fell down the stairs yesterday."

My teacher took me to the nurse's office, and the nurse asked me the same thing: *"What happened to you?"*

"I fell down the stairs yesterday." Yes, I held firm to the lie.

Minutes later, the nurse pulled out a camera and started taking pictures of my horrific injuries. She obviously did not believe me, either.

The following morning, there was a knock on our door. On the other side was the police and a woman from Child Protective Services (CPS). My mother was arrested for child abuse, and my sister and I were placed into CPS custody. My sister was upset and blamed me for the separation. *"You got our mama taken away from us!"* I ignored her because she had no idea about the level of pain I was going through. The weeks flew by. Eventually, we were released to go back home…to mama.

My mother never discussed what happened. Not the abuse. Not her arrest. Not our temporary separation. I never did, either. However, I did keep the incidents stored in the recesses of my heart and mind as I grew up. Again: I will never forget.

Growing up in a strict household was unbearable. For whatever reason, I was the one who seemed to get into the most trouble, which led to me receiving the most abuse. Why? I will never know. My sister never got beatings — and she was the one who used to pick on me **ALL** the time in our home! I hated being at home. Instead, I wanted to spend time at my cousin's house, which was my haven away from my mother and sister. As the years went by, the beatings were fewer.

Only God Knows…Why!!!

For reasons unknown, I never felt loved by my mother nor my sister. I recall my sister making me get into it with her friends just so her friends and I would fight. Another time I remember was when I lost hair in the back of my head. It was then I discovered my sister put Comet cleaner and Clorox bleach into my pink hair moisturizer. One morning, I woke up to a knife at my neck. She wanted to kill me! Why did she hate me so much?! Each time she mistreated me, all I could think was that when I grew up, I would stay my distance from her.

I kept myself busy by becoming actively engaged in the church. At an early age, I accepted the Lord in my life. I joined the choir and drill team, too. Going to church every Sunday was my focus.

After graduating from Dick Dowling Middle School, I knew I wanted to break free from the people I grew up with. When I entered my 9th-grade year, though, I felt so out of place because I did not have everyone else's stylish clothes. I managed to make it through that year successfully and entered 10th grade with a better mindset. My self-esteem had blossomed nicely. During the summer, I was offered a job as a Secretary at a home health agency. I was so happy about making my own money to buy the things I desired for myself. I was also accepted into the Stephen F. Austin High School for Teaching Professions.

Early one morning, I remember hearing the phone ring. When my mother answered, I heard her say, *"Yes, this is her."* I went into the room where she was but heard nothing else. All I saw were tears running down her face.

"What's wrong, mama?" I asked.

"Y'all's father passed away two weeks ago," she replied.

My tears joined hers. It was a devastating moment because my mother was preparing to take my sister and me to Dallas to meet our father for the first time. Before his death, he wrote us letters weekly and often apologized for not being there for us like he should have been. I accepted his apology and forgave him. I hoped to meet my father, see how he looked, hear his voice in person, and hug him. In no way, shape, or form did I ever imagine him dying two weeks before we were scheduled to meet. I suppose it was not meant to be.

Still, I have so many unanswered questions. I have a stepbrother I talk to, but I do not feel comfortable enough asking him questions about our father. His wife would have been the one to ask my laundry list of questions, but she is no longer here, either. There will always be a void in my life that should have been filled by my father. Not knowing much about him hurts the most.

There was, however, a lesson I learned along the way: I vowed never to allow my children not to know anything about their fathers—and **THAT** is no lie. Oddly enough, my story takes an out-of-control twist regarding that very subject.

Chapter Four

My First Thug Love

My 10th-grade year was fun. My school was close to the Third Ward neighborhood of Houston, and I met a lot of cool people, including my first love. I was so happy to meet him, and he showed me a lot of attention. With me being from Hiram Clarke—a totally different atmosphere and part of the city from his—I did not know anyone else from his area.

I recall the first day he approached me. I was instantly flattered. Then, months went by, and I did not see him. I later learned he went to jail for selling drugs. In all my youthful innocence, I did not quite understand what that meant. I knew what it was after reaching out to his mom and sister, who took me to see him in jail every day. I hid the fact that I was visiting him from my mom. (*She thought I was at basketball practice.*)

When he was released from jail, I decided to spend the night with him—but purposely failed to tell my mother. The next day, she went to my school looking for me, but I was not there. My best friend called to tell me about my mother's pop-up visit. I told my boyfriend, who then told his mom. She replied, *"You got her in trouble. She will have to live with us now."*

The next day, I went home to pack up my clothes and other belongings. When my mother asked where I had been, I told her the truth. She replied, *"If you want to be with that **thug**, you can't stay here!"* Basically, she kicked me out. I was only 15 years old at the time. Nonetheless, I was happy about that. I would not have to deal with her and my sister anymore.

So, I left. I packed my clothes and never looked back. I did not call home, either. I was free! *Or was I…*

I barely went to school, choosing to work at Wendy's instead. My boyfriend's mother made sure I went to work when I was on the schedule. I am grateful for the love she showed me.

During our relationship, my boyfriend was in and out of jail. When his mother started getting sick, she told me in confidence that she was diagnosed with throat cancer. She instructed me not to tell my boyfriend and to keep it between her and me. As she got sicker and sicker, I dropped out of school to ensure she received the proper care she deserved. Months later, she died. It broke my heart because she was so kind to me and gave me a place to stay. She was the first person I saw die, leaving a stain on my heart for that tragic loss. I helped plan her funeral.

After years of not talking to my mother, I called to let her know about my boyfriend's mother's passing. She kindly sent her sympathy and condolences.

I thought that by my boyfriend losing his mother, he would have gotten his life on the right track. It did not. His behavior got worse, and he was very bitter. Not long after his mother died, he started abusing me and cheating on me. I wanted to return home, but I could not let my mother get the satisfaction of telling me, *"I told you so."* I chose to hang in there and endure the mistreatment until I had enough.

By that time, I was old enough to get my own place, so I moved into the apartments I grew up in: the Aristocrats Apartments. My mother was still there. She lived in the front, and I stayed in the back. By moving close to home, I was able to mend our relationship.

In 1998, I got pregnant. I continued to work all the while. My boyfriend was back in jail, and I was afraid to tell him I was pregnant. I hid my pregnancy from him as long as I could. When I went to see him one time, he somehow knew and hit me during that visit. I was so embarrassed and ashamed. I cried the whole ride home. I called his grandmother *(she and I had a great relationship)* and told her what happened. She was understandably disturbed by his actions.

One day, I decided I wanted to sell drugs to make extra money. I did that for months until the day they had a drug bust, and the police stopped me. I had just purchased a 50-pack from my daughter's father, which was being stored in between my buttocks, and was on my way home. The police put me in the back seat of a patrol car. As soon as the door was shut, I reached for the pack, crushed it into pieces, and threw it underneath the seat. Twenty minutes later, the officer returned to the car and instructed me to step out. A female officer searched me. Of course, by then, I no longer had anything on me. That did not stop my heart from nearly jumping out of my chest, though. I prayed they would not pull back the seat. Thankfully, they did not. When I was asked for and presented my ID, one of the officers said, *"Your address is not around here. We are going to give you a ticket for trespassing."* I took the ticket with gratitude because I could have gotten a drug charge. Plus, I was pregnant and could have ended up having my baby in jail.

That day, I left Third Ward and never went back. God saved me. I know if it were not for Him, things could have gone **ALL** wrong *THAT* day.

Chapter Five

Name Request

A life-changing event occurred on October 23, 1998: I gave birth to my first daughter. My boyfriend was in jail at the time but called his grandmother to relay a message to me:

Name the baby after him.

I was surprised because he knew she was not his child. It is sad to say, but I did not know who her father was. The man I thought was her father turned out not to be. No DNA test was done. Both of us just **knew**. The man who was her father knew he was, but I did not really like him at all, so I never acknowledged him as her father. Per my boyfriend's request, I named her after him.

Years later, I married him while he was still in jail. When he was released, he helped me with her as if she were his daughter. He lived an upstanding life for a while before reverting to his old ways. Back to jail he went!

I was tired of living that way but kept going to see him every weekend. I also kept money on his books to make sure he was okay while locked away…again.

Chapter Six

Purposely Impregnated

I returned to school to get my high school diploma in 2000. In 2001, I went to school to obtain my Medical Assistant diploma and graduated.

Also, in 2001, I got pregnant and had an abortion. I was dating a guy I did not know was married until his wife knocked on my door. That "relationship" ended quickly.

In 2003, I got pregnant with my third child. That was a shocker because I was still married, and my husband was still in jail. At first, I had no idea I was pregnant. I went to the doctor because I was not feeling well, only to learn I was again with child. Lord! I cried because my husband was scheduled to be released very soon. I did not know what to do.

After leaving the clinic, I called my mother and shared the news with her. Oddly enough, she was happy! I was not. I called the father and told him. He was excited! I was not. I told him I was not going to have it. Here is the thing: He knew I was expecting my husband to come home. He put a hole in the condom and purposely impregnated me. I was so upset! I already had it all planned out, though. I was going to have another abortion.

Time went by, and I hid the pregnancy. When I was around three months along, I made an appointment to have an ultrasound. My mother went with me that day. On the spot, we were told I was carrying a boy. Again, my mother was happy. She was thrilled about her first grandson. As for me, I was devastated. I was quiet the entire way home.

The next morning, I woke up and started to call around to get pricing for an abortion. I kept getting outrageous amounts because I was so far along. At every turn, each clinic informed me of the risks. I ignored them all. My mind was made up.

My mother begged me not to do it. I told her I had to do it. *"Just give him to me,"* she pleaded. *"I will raise him as my son."*

"No," I replied firmly. *"I am not having him."*

After a couple of days went by, I decided to keep him — and to keep him a secret. A month later, my husband was released. I never told him I was pregnant. A month after his release, I went to the doctor, came home, and told my husband I was pregnant *(as if I had just gotten pregnant)*. He believed me, and that was all that mattered. When I gave birth to my son, I pretended he was birthed prematurely. Again, my husband believed it.

Sometime later, he questioned me while the baby and I were still in the hospital. *"Is that baby really mine?"*

"Yes," I said with more confidence than I had.

He left the hospital and returned with all kinds of baby items. My son was named after him that very day.

Months later, he went back to jail. It was then I had the courage to tell him in writing that my son was not his. He was so hurt, which did nothing to help his behavior while outside of a jail cell. As for me, I was tired of him doing whatever he wanted to do whenever he wanted to do it when he was not behind bars. It was time for me to get my life in order.

Chapter Seven

My Body, My Mind, My Choice

In 2007, I left my husband for good. I then started talking to and dating my friend who had a shoulder I used to cry on about my husband. He and I spent a lot of time together and wouldn't you know it? I ended up getting pregnant!

After tiring of him ignoring my calls for days on end, I went to his apartment to inform him he would be a father. His brother answered the door and told me, *"He hasn't been here in a couple of days."* Worry set in, but I also knew he had a history of being addicted to drugs.

Almost immediately, I scheduled and had an abortion. No one knew. I kept it a secret. Days later, after I regained my strength, I returned to his apartment. Again, his brother answered and said my boyfriend was not home. I then showed the brother the document that stated I had an abortion. His brother put his head down in disbelief. I turned and walked away.

Although I was hurt because of what I did, I knew I did not want to raise another child by myself. It was already a challenge, and I was tired of the sacrifices I had to make, including working more than one job to make ends meet to care for my children alone. I had no help from their fathers, so I knew I made the right choice for me in my heart. Months later, he came back around, and I told him what happened. He was hurt, but I explained to him why I made that choice.

A year later, in 2008, I got pregnant by him again. We were together at the time. He even went through the entire pregnancy with me, including all the doctor's appointments. Finally! One of my children's fathers was in their life in the same household!

In 2009, he did his disappearing act. I thought he was dead for sure when I did not hear from him. He eventually contacted me to let me know he was in jail. He called and asked about his daughter often. When he was out of jail, he kept in touch with her and, whenever he would stop indulging in his addiction to go into recovery, I made sure he was able to see her, even if it took me holding her up in the air while he looked out a window. I did my part as her mother because I knew he was never a part of his other child's life.

Chapter Eight

The Birthing of a Vision

In 2010, I finally put my foot down and went on with my life. That same year, I officially divorced my first husband. It was also the year God gave me a vision. I did not know what to make of it at first, so I wrote down everything I saw in the vision.

There was a pregnant woman in a house. I jumped on Google to see what I could make of that piece of the vision. Through research and discernment, I learned God wanted me to open a maternity home. Shortly after, I came up with a name: **God's Lovely Butterflies Maternity Home.**

Through the organization, we help teen mothers and single mothers with essential items for their babies. When needed, we also help them obtain their GED, provide parenting and computer classes, and take them to doctor's appointments. Once they leave the maternity home, they have the skills necessary to survive on their own. They can take care of their children and be productive mothers.

Chapter Nine

No! Not My Babies!

In 2012, my daughter's father wanted his family back. I gave him another chance—a decision my family was not at all happy with. I thought it was a good choice because he was a good provider. Everything I wanted, he gave me.

We got married, and no one from my family or circle of friends came to the wedding. My mother did not even come. The only people who represented me on my side were the ones **in** the wedding. His family and friends were there, as happy as they could be. I recall some of his family sitting on my side to make it "look full."

We did not even manage to stay married for a year. I thought he had changed his old ways, but he did not, which caused us to get into it often. In 2013, we separated for good.

Months later, I received a call from CPS stating they received a report that they had to act on. I was freaked out and worried at the same time. *"Who called CPS on me?"* I wondered. I went to the office, and they shared the allegation with me. They also informed me my children would have to be removed from my home. When they asked if I had a family member they could go to, I knew my mother could not help me out because she had a CPS case of her own with me that would have disqualified her. I gave them my godmother's name and phone number. When I left the building, I immediately called my godmother, explained what happened, and told her to be on the lookout for a call from CPS. The agency called her and asked if she was willing to care for my children until I took parenting classes, to which she agreed.

I was distraught. I could not bear the thought of being away from my children for any length of time.

CPS also had to speak with my youngest daughter's father because we were living together. That was yet another challenge because he did not like my family at all. He was not in agreement with his daughter going to my godmother's house and stated he wanted his child to go to his mother's home. His mother and I never saw eye-to-eye. She always said my daughter was not his child. Even after taking a paternity test and it came back 99.9% positive that she was his, his mother said that I could have changed the results because I worked at a doctor's office.

Why would I do that?! If I wanted to, I could have chosen **ANYONE** to be my daughter's father if that were the case!

Needless to say, his family refused to take on the responsibility, so our daughter had to stay with my godmother. He was so upset, but there was nothing he could do about it. When he visited our daughter, he never wanted to follow the rules. He always caused scenes and acted out of order. Although he, too, was ordered to take parenting classes, he never did.

As for me, I cried virtually every day that my children were not with me. I could visit them, but they were not permitted to go anywhere with me or spend the night. That situation was the hardest thing I have ever dealt with, but I did what I had to do to get my children back. I took the ordered classes and completed them in the allotted time. Several months later, my children were back home with me.

After all the hell I went through to regain custody of my children and having to deal with CPS, I knew I never wanted to be with my daughter's father again in my life. I loved my children and never wanted them to be apart from me again, so I made it my business to focus on them and getting my life in order from that point forward. My children being taken away from me was a major scare. I could have lost my children to "the system"! My life would have been worthless because they were the reason I remained motivated.

During our time together, my husband cheated on me and flirted with most of my friends. My **REAL** friends denied his advances. The *FAKE* ones chose to stab me in the back because he had money, and they tried to get in where they thought they could fit in. He knew he could not destroy me, so he tried everything under the sun to get under my skin.

One time, he took our daughter away from me and worked hard to make others think I was an unfit mother. I did not talk to my child for months, which crushed my heart. I had no idea where she was. When the time came for me to meet him, he played games and was a no-show.

After tiring of his antics, I decided to get an attorney to fight for divorce and full custody. To attain the money needed for the attorney's fees, I reached out to people who helped me organize a fundraiser. Much to my disappointment, that was a waste of time and money. The attorney seemed to be more on my ex's side than actually representing me.

For example, when we went to mediation, my ex was awarded all my furniture — the same furniture I had before he and I got together. I lost it all. When I left, he would not let me take any of my things except for my clothes. Just when I wanted to give up the fight for my daughter, he gave her back to me. I will never forget how tightly she held me and would not let me out of her eyesight for some time after our reunion.

Once on our own and away from him, we had a hard time getting settled. My children and I slept on the floor until I could afford a bed. It was challenging finding a place to live because my credit was not the best. One day, I grabbed a Greensheet newspaper and found a house. I called the owner, asked to see the home, and arranged a meeting. Honestly, I did not know how I would pay my rent and bills, but I was honored by the chance he gave me.

I stayed in that home for four years. I know it was God showering me with His favor that day. It was only He who made a way out of no way.

Chapter Ten

Remembering Mama

FINALLY! In 2014, I was granted my second divorce. I was elated because I could finally close that chapter of my life—the one that hurt me the most. I believe the marriage was the worst anyone could go through. Time after time, he set me up to catch cases with the judicial system so that I would lose custody of my children. His efforts were fruitless, though. Things worked out in my favor because the cases were dismissed.

HOWEVER...

Having those charges connected to me was horrific. Assault and terroristic cases he brought against me did some damage to my credibility for a while. I could not get good jobs and had to settle for ones I did not want. I had to do what I had to do to care for my three children.

In 2015, my mother had a horrible stroke and never fully recovered. She needed help around the clock, so I had to stop working to provide for her needs. I was left alone to make decisions for her because my sister was not active in the process like we needed her to be. To give my mother the best possible care, I put everything my mother did to me in the past to the side. It was a hard task with a lot of sleepless nights.

There came a time when the doctors wanted to amputate her legs due to a lack of circulation. I did not know what to do other than pray. The answer to my prayers came when the cardiologist called me and said he decided against performing the surgery because my mother was too weak. Months later, she died. I was right by her side to the very end.

My heart was at peace. I did all I could to take care of her in her time of need in her last days. She suffered a lot, and I would not dare like to witness her continuing to endure all she went through. She was on a feeding tube. She could not talk. She was in severe pain. There are moments when I cry because I miss her, but God needed her back.

No matter how our relationship was, I was able to rise above our circumstances and be the one there for her when she needed me the most. Before she passed, I told her I forgave her and begged for her forgiveness for my wrongdoings. At the end of the day, she was my one and only mother. I had to honor her for that if nothing else. After all, she took care of me and took on the responsibility of raising my twin and me without our father's help.

Chapter Eleven

Happy Days Are Here Again!

The year was 2015. After deciding a serious relationship was not for me, I spent time just talking to other guys and made some great male friends along the way. My trust issues kept me from desiring to get involved with anyone, so I learned to enjoy my own company the best.

That was until…

I met a man at the apartments where I grew up who needed my notary services. He started flirting with me, but I did not pay him much attention. My mind simply was not in that space. Well, a couple of days later, we went out on a date. We had a wonderful time, and I genuinely enjoyed myself.

As the months passed, we started getting closer. When he proposed to me, I said yes. We set a date for the wedding: April 16, 2016. I was happy about finally finding someone whom I loved and who loved me back. We began to plan our wedding together excitedly. For the first time in a **LONG** time, both my children and family were happy as well. I met his family when we went to North Carolina, and I liked them all from the start.

Sometime later, I received a mysterious message in my inbox from a woman asking when the wedding was. She went on to say she wanted to buy me a wedding gift because she saw that I do so much for the community. I was puzzled. I thought to myself, *"This does not sound right at all."* I then snooped through her photos on social media and stumbled across a picture of my fiancé's car before he fixed it up, so I sent him a screenshot of the conversation I had with the mystery woman. That was followed up by a phone call with me, asking, *"Who is she?"*

He replied, *"My ex."*

"The one who was in the military?"

"Yes."

I was really confused. *"Why is she trying to come to our wedding?"*

"I don't know," he said, sounding just as perplexed.

I ended up blocking her and chose never to respond further. She never reached out to me again.

Chapter Twelve

The Flip-Flopped Surprise

As we continued to plan for our big day, I kept a close eye on my health. I made sure I went for my annual checkup and well-woman exam. Imagine my surprise when I received a call from my doctor telling me I need to begin taking antibiotics for a Sexually-Transmitted Disease (STD)!

When I called to tell my fiancé about the STD and was going to be prescribed medication to treat it, he reminded me he did not have insurance to do the same. That following morning, I went to the free clinic and told them I wanted to be checked for STDs, just so I could get him some medication to take as well.

While at the clinic, they offered to give me an HIV/AIDS test. I was okay with taking it because just six months prior, I was tested, and the results came back negative. As I waited patiently for all the testing results, I was told they needed to counsel me.

"I already know I have an STD," I said.

"Yes, but we have something else to counsel you about."

Well, that piqued my curiosity for sure. I went to the back for the counseling session. The conversation went from zero to 100 in the blink of an eye.

Counselor: *"How are you?"*

Me: *"I'm okay."*

Counselor: *"Sorry to inform you, Mrs. Kearney, but your test for HIV came back positive."*

Me: ***"No way!"*** Did she really just come out and say it like **THAT**?! When I was shown the results, I froze in place. I could not even cry because I was numb.

She asked me about my sex partners, and I told her I only had one in the last year. She stated she needed to know about my previous ones as well, so I gave her the names. She went on to say they must be tested as well.

Me (to myself): *"Uh oh. That will not go well at all."*

The counselor asked for the name of the most recent person I had sex with and how long we were dating. I gave her his name and told her we have been dating for a little over six months. She said he would need to be tested as well.

I felt my body going into a state of shock. My mind went back to my ex-husband. I just knew he was the one who gave it to me. When I left the clinic that day, I called three of my good friends and told them about the clinic visit. All of them cried with and for me. Once home, I cried some more. Thankfully, my fiancé was at work at the time. I was so scared to tell him about the results and did not do so for about a week.

One day, I called my fiancé while he was at work and told him we needed to talk. He listened attentively as I started crying and explained the reason for my tears.

"Remember the day I went to the doctor to get medication for you?"

"Yes."

"That day, I was informed that I have HIV."

The silence that followed was deafening. He started crying and ended the call. Shortly after, he came through the door of our home, and we cried together. I told him what the clinic told me: *"They will call me to set up a place for further testing."* I could not wait on them, though, so I started Googling places in the area and found one on Thomas Street. I called and made an appointment for both of us.

That day, my appointment time was before his. As they checked me out, they asked, *"Did you bring your partner?"* I replied that I did. After swabbing his mouth, his results came back positive for HIV as well. I dropped my head guiltily, just knowing I gave it to him because of my ex-husband's lifestyle on the streets. My ex's bad choices could have cost me my life and the life of the man I love! The clinic did a blood draw from both of us and scheduled us to return in two weeks.

The ride home that day was eerily quiet. I did not talk much because I was really scared, angry at my ex, and heartbroken because I gave the disease to my fiancé. I could tell he was sad and in deep thought as well.

When the two weeks had finally passed, we went back to the clinic to meet with the doctor. She went over our results together and stated my numbers were good, meaning it seemed like a new case.

Wait. What? **NEW?** I thought I had it and gave it to him. Talk about confused!

As she discussed his results, she said his numbers were extremely high and that he was one point away from having full-blown AIDS. Tears immediately welled up in my eyes. I had to leave the room. I felt my heart growing heavy with despair. I made my way to the bathroom and cried my eyes out before returning to the room with my fiancé and the doctor.

Doctor: *"Are you okay?"*

Me: *"No."*

Doctor: *"Would you like for me to scheduled you to see a therapist?"*

Me: *"Yes."*

Before leaving, the doctor scheduled my appointment with the therapist, wrote the referral, and prescribed both of our medications, which we filled immediately at the pharmacy located downstairs from the clinic.

Chapter Thirteen

Just A Week Ago…

I learned of my diagnosis one week before I was going to get married. **Lord, WHY?** What was I supposed to do with that newfound information?

When I first opened the medicine bottle and saw how big the pill was, my depression seemed to deepen even more. My fiancé came over to comfort me and said, *"I am so sorry you must go through this. I am so sorry."*

However, what I **'heard'** in his apology was, *"I am so sorry. I did not know I had it. I'm sorry this happened to you."* I was hurt and confused. I cried almost every day after that. As for him, he seemed to handle the news quite well. He barely mentioned another word about it. He simply continued with his daily routine like nothing was wrong. If he could do it, so could I.

I released the hurt and still married him on what seemed like the happiest day of my life. We were surrounded by family and friends, including his people from North Carolina. The event was standing room only. Everyone was so happy for us.

I am grateful I did not let my hurt get in the way of our special day. I had a certain level of comfort in knowing I, too, had the strength to go on as if nothing life-changing happened just one week prior.

Chapter Fourteen

Lies, Deceit…and Facebook

A month after saying our *"I Dos,"* my husband told me there was an upcoming weekend trip he had planned to go to Austin with his friends that was made before we got married. He sounded sincere when he told me he did not really want to go but did not want to lose out on the money he already spent. I agreed with his logic and said, *"That's fine."*

The weekend came, and before he left, he assured me he would call to let me know when he arrived. I never received that call. Instead, I received a three-word text message:

"We made it."

I thought to myself, *"Your homeboys know you just got married, so surely they would want you to check in with your wife."* That entire weekend, I had an uneasy feeling. He called home one time while he was away, with that one call filled with a lot of background noise. I could not hear him whatsoever. He never called back.

That Sunday, he returned home. Now, mind you, that funny feeling that he was not doing right by me while he was away remained. The first opportunity I had, I grabbed his phone and went into my office. Since I knew the code to his phone, I unlocked it, went through his texts, and called the last number dialed. A woman answered.

"This is Darlene. Who is this?" I demanded.

She told me her name and went on to explain she was the woman who sent me that message on Facebook about the wedding and bringing me a gift.

I asked, *"Were you and my husband together this weekend?"*

"Yes. He went with my daughter and me to a track meet."

My heart dropped. I quickly ended the call and then phoned one of my best friends to tell her about what happened. She was also one of the few who knew about my HIV positive status. She was appalled and instructed me to make a three-way call with her, the other woman, and me. When the call connected, my friend immediately told the woman about my husband's status and asked her if she knew. I then asked, *"Did you see him taking medication while he was there?"*

She replied, *"Yes, I did. He said it was his blood pressure medicine."*

I then sent her a photo of his pill bottle and diagnosis from his medical records from our clinic visit. She claimed she did not know. I suggested she get herself checked out. I even offered to go with her, but she kept making excuses not to meet up with me. A few days passed, and she sent me an image of a test she took. It looked like something she pulled from the internet. I asked her to let me see the hardcopy, to which she replied, *"I do not have it."* Until this day, I do not know if she has HIV/AIDS because she has yet to say. In my heart, I believe she does because she and my husband dated three years before he and I met.

Moving along...

He and I worked through that instance of his cheating. I forgave him and dropped the subject. His deceit did not end there, though. We went on a trip to his hometown. What he did not know was that I knew the password to his Facebook account. While his cousin and I went to the store, my husband started messaging two of his exes, not knowing I saw every word. He was trying to meet up with them! When we made it back to his aunt's house, I went **OFF** on him. I wanted to leave right then and there but chose to stay…and forgive him yet again for his "indiscretion." On our return trip home, we took turns driving. During one of his times in the driver's seat, he asked me to upload some pictures from the weekend to his tablet. It was then I saw a message from one of his exes. Apparently, he had sent her a message, and she responded. Because I wanted to make it home safely, I kept what I knew to myself.

Once home, I went **OFF** for the second time in as many days. I asked why he sent his ex a message. He, of course, denied it. What I later learned, however, was that while I was inside at the homecoming reunion with his family, he was talking to her. Although I was livid, I forgave him for that, too.

Chapter Fifteen

A Funny Feeling

Sometime later, I started having problems with my landlord. I owed him late fees for the rent. He told me he would work with me, which he did at first—until he found out I moved my husband in with me. He then took me to court and demanded I vacate the premises.

The rent was due a couple of days after our appearance, so I paid it with the hopes that he would give me a break. He did not. He took the rent money and **still** handed me a three-day vacate notice.

I was so angry and felt helpless. I did not know what to do. Of course, the only choice was to move, so I started packing up and moving things to storage. In one weekend, we emptied and moved out of a four-bedroom house. It was hard, but we did it. We had no place to go with such short notice, so my husband and I stayed in a hotel room for three months until I could save up for another house. My children stayed with my godmother during that time. It was heartbreaking being away from my children and having to wake up early to take them to school each day, but I did it because I had to. I was just waiting for my breakthrough.

Finally, we were approved for a house. It was a three-bedroom, although I wanted four—but hey, beggars cannot be choosy. I was tired of staying in that hotel room and eating fast-food every night.

We moved in, and things started getting better for us. In my spirit, I felt he was doing right. I then started a fast to get clarification on what direction I wanted our relationship to go, especially after having my feelings hurt time and again by him. Months passed, and I went to church one Sunday with my youngest daughter. He chose not to attend service with us that day. Once again, a funny feeling set in. After church, I called him. No answer. I then sent a text. He did not reply until about 30 minutes later:

"I'm at BreWings watching the game."

"Which one?" I asked. No response whatsoever came.

I then Googled his ex's phone number, and her address came up with a home-based business she had. I got in my car, put the address into the GPS, and pulled into the apartments. There sat his truck. I sent another text:

"Which BreWings are you at?" No response. I was persistent. My next text read, *"One of my friends said she saw you there with a woman."*

That stirred a response. *"I'm with her cousin."*

I had enough of his games and lies. I parked my car and climbed into his truck. I never told him I had a copy of his key, so imagine his surprise when he exited the apartment and saw his vehicle was gone. He called and called and called, but I refused to answer. Once home, I started packing his clothes. About an hour later, his uncle brought him home. By then, I was fuming and told his uncle everything I knew, including that his nephew was HIV positive. His uncle seemed genuinely surprised, grabbed his nephew, and left.

I breathed a huge sigh of relief, packed up all his clothes in his truck, and drove it back to his ex's apartment complex. He was upset, but I thought to myself, *"OH WELL!"*

Chapter Sixteen

Ten Tees

When I returned home that day, I typed up my divorce papers and filed them the next day. He did not want to sign them, so he gave me a difficult time. Eventually, he did, and we were divorced in 2017.

You might not be surprised to learn he moved back in with his ex, all while begging me daily to take him back. I was determined not to let him back into my life. I was sick and tired of being sick and tired—literally. My heart was weak, though. Months later, we started talking again. Shortly after, he moved back in with me, and we were okay for a while.

One day, he came home acting as if he were drunk. When I went through his phone, I saw where he had texted his ex that he had made it home. At that moment, as I reflected on the events of that day, I put it all together. That explained why, while I was out with my beautician eating crawfish, he kept calling to see where I was and asking how long it would be before I made it home. He was cheating on me again with **HER**! I immediately kicked him out. One other mistake I made was having his name tattooed on me. I quickly rectified that situation by going to Daggos and getting a cover-up tattoo.

We got back together…again. We were well into 2018 by that time.

I recall asking him to take me down the street to get a phone number for the new houses that were being built in the neighborhood. His car was parked on the street, so I suggested taking his car. I noticed his hesitation. I went around to the driver's side. He opened the passenger's side door, grabbed a bag, and quickly threw it into the back seat, hoping I would not notice. I did. The whole time we were out, I wondered what he had in the bag that he did not want me to see.

Once back in the house, I received a call from a mother who needed some baby items, so I left to go to my office. I never told him I was leaving. When I returned, I noticed he still had his car keys with him. It was unusual because he always put them on the counter. Later, one of my friends came by, so I went outside to talk to her. After she left, I went back inside and noticed he placed the keys on the counter as usual. I then grabbed my phone and went outside to look for the bag, but it was not there. A different bag sat in its place. I went back inside, got his keys, found the other bag in the trunk, opened it, and saw about ten t-shirts inside. I took a picture with my phone and sent him a text with it that asked, *"Why are you hiding shirts?"* I waited for a response that never came. I refused to be ignored.

I went into the house and went **OFF** on him. I ended with, *"You have to **LEAVE**!"* I grabbed his keys to remove my house key. Before I could complete the task, he grabbed them out of my hand, pushed me outside, jumped into his car, and left. My left hand was bruised from the "altercation." I called the police. They came and filed a report. When I was asked if I wanted to file charges against him, I said *"YES!"* without hesitation. However, I never did pursue those charges.

That incident was the straw that broke the camel's back. I was finally at my end. Dealing with him was too much drama and trauma. Until that moment, I felt that I had to be with him because of the "gift" he gave me. I felt obligated to him and believed I had to put up with his crap.

When I finally embraced my self-worth, I understood my purpose in his life: God sent me to save him. Were it not for me and my early-stage HIV diagnosis, he would likely not have known he was one point away from having full-blown AIDS.

Chapter Seventeen

Think First, React Later

For three years, I tried hanging in there with him. I thought he would get a mindset to eventually change his life, mostly because he was six years older than I was. He never did change.

I could no longer sit around and wait for him to change. Life is too short. I deserve to be happy. I deserve to be loved. I deserve a faithful man because I am a faithful woman. I cannot continue to put my life at risk for him.

Every day of my life, I take my medication and am reminded of what he did to me. I do not hate him, as I played a part in my fate. Still, it is as if he has no remorse for **HIS** part in my future.

What remains puzzling to me is that he continued getting caught cheating with his ex. The last time I caught him was on a Friday. I was lying in my bed, tired from working two full-time jobs. I remember it being a Friday because that day was my day of rest. I checked my phone and saw I had a missed call from him, so I returned his call—twice. No answer. I got up, put on my clothes, and got into my car, heading toward his ex-girlfriend's house *(the same one he was always caught cheating with)*. When I made it to the area, I mistakenly turned onto the wrong street, so I made a U-turn and turned onto the correct one. Much to my surprise, his car was coming down the street from the opposite direction with a passenger in tow. He turned into the driveway, and I pulled up behind his car on the street so that he could see me. He had his ex in his car! I had nothing to say. I felt numb. There was so much I wanted to say, but the words would not come out. She got out of the car, hit the garage opener button, and entered her house through the garage. He put his car in reverse, so I moved forward a bit so that he could back out. He then pulled up beside my car. I spoke one word, and that was, *"Really?"* Tears rolled down my cheeks as I put my car in drive and drove away in tears.

I began to thank God for allowing me to see that man's cheating ways with my own eyes. I also thanked God for letting me stay calm and to first think about my children, career, and businesses. That day, I asked God to please give me the strength to leave that man alone.

After that day, my ex called and called. I answered when I wanted to, which was not very often. When I did answer, I told him how I felt and that I had no more fight in me.

"It's not what you thought," he said. *"I took her to get a part for her car."*

I replied, *"Really? You take her to get a part, yet I have been waiting for you to fix one of my vehicles that has been down for **months**!"*

"I was thinking about the money," he said, surely believing his own lie.

"Okay," I replied and then hung up.

I said to myself, *"I cannot let him continue to hurt me. I have been hurt by him since the day we met. He has no intention of doing the right things."* Obviously, he did not care that he continued to hurt me time and time again with the same person over and over.

I had to get to a point where I was tired of dealing with his cheating, lies, and manipulation. Only then could I leave him alone once and for all. That day came when I realized my worth. I spoke life to myself:

"Darlene, you do not have to settle for anything less than what you deserve in your life. God loves you, and He made you. He wrote your life. What you are enduring was in His plans for your life before you were formed in your mother's womb."

Listen, I know that accepting what God allows to happen can be difficult at times. I have cried silent cries and have moments when I want to question God and ask Him, **"WHY???"** Many nights, I have cried and asked, *"**WHY** can't I feel love like everyone else???"* I have yearned for love throughout my life because I did not feel like my mother loved me. I grew up believing she loved my twin sister more, even though I was her firstborn.

Sadly, I never had a chance to ask my mother what I wanted to before her passing. Instead, I chose to keep those questions bottled up inside. I implore you not to do the same.

Chapter Eighteen

Family Tragedy

In 2018, I decided to go back to school to become a Substance Abuse Counselor. That choice was a product of the alcohol addiction my cousin suffered from as a result of the tragic loss of her only daughter, who died in a house fire in 2007. She turned to alcohol to relieve her pain.

I pray for her often because she has yet to recover from the loss of her only child. My baby cousin was an 18-year-old high school graduate when God called her home. The one thing that remains in my mind was how, the day before she died, my older children were playing in the other room, and I heard them mention her name. They said they wished she could come to the house for the summer *(she often visited us in Houston during the summer and holidays)*.

I remember getting a call around 3:00 a.m. from one of my cousins the day my cousin died. I could tell by her voice that something was wrong. She asked if I was home alone, and I said that I was. She hesitated before saying, *"We had a family tragedy. There was a housefire in Jeanerette. Everyone made it out except for our little cousin."* I dropped the phone and started crying uncontrollably. At that moment, I had so many questions, but I kept them to myself until I could find out what happened.

I learned my cousin woke up her mom, grandmother, and grandfather while yelling, *"FIRE!"* She died from smoke inhalation. To my understanding, the source of the fire was electrical. Her loss was a tragedy to the entire family. She died on one of my cousin's birthdays, so that day will be one our family will never forget.

I was unable to attend her funeral because I was in the middle of doing a research study. I would rather remember her the way she was when I last saw her. I hated, however, that I could not be there for my family. My cousin knew my heart. I loved her so much. As a matter of fact, my youngest daughter has my cousin's name as her middle name. She will never be forgotten.

Chapter Nineteen

The Top of the World

In May 2018, I graduated from the Substance Abuse Counselor course. What a significant accomplishment for me to have finally completed something in life! I took six classes at a time to finish school early. Because of my disability, I was able to get a full scholarship for school. DARS (Department of Assistive and Rehabilitative Services) paid for my classes and books. I was so grateful for the friend who introduced me to the program. I never knew about that resource until then. I used it to my benefit to get the help I needed for school because I could not receive financial aid. I had exhausted my lifetime credit for financial aid because of previous attempts to go to school but not completing the course. That time, I had it in my mind to finish.

While working at the jail, I saw a counselor assessing a client and thought to myself, *"That is what I really want to do."* I signed up for the classes *(passing them all)*, went to school full-time, and worked a full-time job. Juggling it all was hard, but I was driven by the need to be and do more for my children and me. The effort had to be put forth to achieve my goal.

The day I heard my name and walked across the stage was the best feeling ever. I felt on top of the world! A few family members and friends came to share that special day with me. Most importantly, my children were there, and I knew my mother was smiling down on me from Heaven. I was so proud of myself for pushing my way through. There were days I did not feel well. There was the time I lost two cousins back-to-back during the last semester. When taking my final, I received a text from my oldest daughter, stating I was not a good mother. It was evident to me the enemy did not want me to be great. The devil wanted me to break and have me thinking I was not good enough, but I maintained my focus—and I excelled!

I had to send my paperwork to the State office to get approved. The wait for a response was excruciating! I checked daily for the status of my application. I must admit: I was concerned because of my background and the three criminal charges that seemed to make appearances when least expected: Criminal Mischief, Assault, and Terroristic Threat. Even though the Assault and Terroristic Threat charges were dismissed, I was still afraid they would interfere with my future. I feared being denied the opportunity I worked so hard to achieve.

Two months later, my application was approved. Thank You, Jesus! I knew my clearance was coming in the mail, so I started filling out applications and going on interviews. I was denied twice. I did not give up, though. I posted my resume on Indeed.com, and about a week later, I received a call from a job I had applied for earlier that week. The interview was on my mother's birthday: July 10th.

I GOT THE JOB! Glory to God! I was overjoyed about being able to work towards my required 4,000 hours!

In the past, I worked two jobs to maintain. Working long hours and two full-time jobs was overwhelming at times, but I thought of my children and the fact that I was their only provider. I had to continue working two jobs to compensate for the lack of financial support received. Not only did I work, but I also had businesses of my own to help make extra money.

One day, I know I will have the desires of my heart, for the Bible tells me so.

I appreciate everything I have in life because I have worked diligently to get it.

Chapter Twenty

The Not-So-Perfect Life

My life is not perfect. It definitely has its challenges. One thing I have been dealing with for years concerns my son. He has Attention Deficit Hyperactivity Disorder (ADHD)—a condition he's had since kindergarten. He has been kicked out of multiple schools because of his disorder. It has been so overwhelming. It is hard raising a son on my own. Many of my most challenging times as a single mother have been on account of him. I have cried countless tears and felt helpless many days.

It does not help that I cannot be stressed out due to my own health issues.

Talking to him seems to sometimes fall on deaf ears. I remember one time when I tried to get him help, and he jumped out of the car, trying to commit suicide. I ran behind him, dodging cars, but he got away. I had to call the police for help. When they found my son, they took him to Ben Taub Hospital. From there, he was admitted to a behavioral hospital, where he stayed for one week to help him with his medication regimen. He was upset with me for putting him there, but I had to. He gave me no choice.

When he came home, he did very well for a while. Then, he went back to disrespecting his teachers and acting out in school. He was suspended time and time again. I was grateful for the school's willingness to work with him and not kick him out because I knew it would be hard for him to get into another school with the behavioral problems he had.

There are times when he lashes out at me and says hurtful things. I try not to let those moments get to me. Still, words do hurt, especially when you know you are trying your best. I realize he is a teenager with teen issues. We have all "been there, done that." Plus, he still hasn't healed from the death of my mother.

Discipline often comes in the form of me taking away his gaming system — something he hates me doing. It is hard to discipline him, though, when outsiders are in his ear *(family members)*. Instead of telling my son the right things to do, they encourage his wrong behaviors.

One thing I have learned along the way is not to let anyone take me out of my character. I have learned not to let things get to me like they used to. I simply remove myself from the situation. I may not always want to do that, but it is best for my health. Learning to love from a distance is healthy at times.

Daily, we are losing our sons to the streets. I never want **my** son to end up in jail. I saw too many young men in the facility where I used to work. As for my son, I pray every day for his protection and guidance.

Chapter Twenty-One

Parents Never Give Up

All I have been through cannot be contained to just one book. The trials and tribulations I have endured might have made an average person give up. Although I have never tried to kill myself, I have had thoughts of harming myself. Whenever those types of thoughts come to mind, I think about my children and how they would have no one to help them along life's journey.

I often wonder how their fathers can go through any given day and not at least check on them to see if they are okay. **Who does that? *WHY?????***

As for me, some days are better than others. If you are a parent, I am sure you would agree with me when I say it is not easy being a parent. The sacrifices we must make for our children can sometimes feel unbearable, but parents never give up. Parenting takes a lot of prayers and needs a strong support system.

I admire and respect those who have stepped in to help me in my time of need. You know who you are, and I thank you.

Chapter Twenty-Two

Total Faith

After seeing my mother have three strokes due to worry and stress, I have learned to pray and fast more often. No longer will I allow things I have no control over to get to me. I choose to push through and give God the glory through it **ALL**. My faith in God is at 100%!

Storms come and go. I have learned to deal with everything that comes my way versus worrying about everything that comes my way.

People will let you down, but God never will. Once you start having total faith in Him, you will witness Him fighting battles for you. For example, in my bitterness, I wanted to hurt anyone and everyone who hurt me, but I did not. In due time, I saw God deal with those individuals in His own, unique way.

The family was sometimes my worst enemy. I had to break away from them, as well. I have endured too much in my life to accept those who mean me no good. Life is too short, and I am on a mission to be the best I can be for God, my children, and me.

Chapter Twenty-Three

A Gentle Tap on My Own Back

I am proud of my accomplishments and have learned that I cannot truly depend on anyone else but myself. Sometimes, I am my only cheerleader, and I am okay with that.

Within the community, I have won several awards for the work I do. It is an amazing feeling to put my mind to something and accomplish the task. Recently I took a test required to sell auto insurance. Next, I will take the test to sell life insurance. I am the proud owner of several businesses. I do it **ALL** for my children. The hustle is **REAL**!

When I leave this earth, my children will not have to depend on anyone. With my legacy, they will be able to say, *"My mother worked hard and did what she had to do to make sure we were wealthy and will not have to ask anyone for anything."*

My mother struggled while raising my sister and me. At the time of her death, she barely had enough for her burial. I had to pitch in to make sure she had a headstone, which was a sacrifice I had to make. I did so without complaining because I was happy to give something back to her for all she had done for me.

Chapter Twenty-Four

Behind My Pretty Smile

There were many days I took risky chances. Overdraft was my best friend at times. I know I could have made things easier for me by applying for housing assistance or finding an apartment I could afford without struggling, but I did not want that for my children and me. More than anything else, I wanted my children to have their own rooms, a back yard they could play in, and a garage for my vehicles.

With my choice came bills…and more bills. I lived from paycheck to paycheck, all while praying nothing would get cut off. There were many times I made payment arrangements just to buy myself some time until my check came through. No one knew my struggle. I hid it well.

No one knew what was hiding behind my pretty smile. I wore a mask because I wanted better than what I could provide.

BUT GOD! I am here today to testify of His grace, mercy, goodness, and lovingkindness!

Chapter Twenty-Five

Drama and Pain Are No More

Once you have endured life's most difficult trials and tribulations, you may find yourself numb to the experience. Things that should hurt you no longer have that effect. People who try to hurt you no longer get under your skin. You learn to distance yourself from those individuals so that they can no longer cause you pain. The older you get, the more you embrace those things that are of the utmost importance, and you make them your focus. At a certain age *(which varies from person to person)*, you do not want to be around drama or painful situations.

I thank God for making me the strong woman I am today. Each circumstance the enemy used to try to kill me proved only to make me stronger. I have forgiven those who hurt me simply because it was the God thing to do.

MESSAGE: When you genuinely forgive others, you can sleep much better at night.

Have you ever wondered why it is that people you give your all to are the ones who seem to hurt you the most? That expression, *"Hurt people hurt people,"* is the **truth**! I have given my all to some who did not deserve it, as proven evident in my past relationships and marriages where I was hurt the most. I know I was not perfect. I will never profess to be. However, I was loyal and gave 100% to the relationships—even when I knew I was not getting the same in return.

I have always trusted my instincts because they never failed me. I recall the comments and questions that followed each failed relationship or marriage.

"Dang! She just got married and already getting a divorce?"

"I told her he was no good."

"How many relationships has she been in?"

"Why does she keep going back?"

As women, we know the signs but often ignore them. Meanwhile, the pain builds, and when we release it, it is like a nuclear explosion! Have you ever had to ask **ANY** of the following questions?

- ➢ *"Why can't he be faithful?"*
- ➢ *"Why can't one woman be enough?"*
- ➢ *"Why hurt the one who has your back?"*
- ➢ *"Why be disrespectful to your wife?"*

Those types of questions will likely never receive an honest answer. I will never knock the few relationships that have a firm, honest, and loving foundation. Some men **ARE** satisfied with one woman. Not **ALL** men cheat.

At the time of this writing, I have not met that man yet. Or maybe I have but feared what others would think of him. I likely thought, *"He's not my type,"* but he was the one who would have given me genuine love, attention, respect, and loved the Lord as I do. That man likely showed an interest in me and prayed for me in a great way, but I ignored my "Mr. Right" because I wanted someone who dressed better and looked better.

Many nights, I have cried out to God and asked, *"What can I possibly be doing wrong to keep having a series of bad men?"* I see my friends happy and wonder when my time will come. When will I find someone who will love and respect me like I desire and deserve? Where is the man who will not play games with my heart, inbox other women, nor meet up with them?

Listen, ladies. Just because that man gives you the world does not mean they are "100" with you. I was showered with everything I wanted by my second husband. I now know they were "guilt gifts." A Hummer. Michael Kors purses. Four-karat rings. An iPad and tablets. Coach and Michael Kors watches. Those things were, of course, nice to have. However, I wanted him to love me like I loved him. There were many nights I risked my life trying to find him when he did his "disappearing act," just to find out he loved drugs more than me. I forgave him, though, and am grateful for the one gift he could never take away: my daughter, Serenity.

Conclusion

Things are finally coming together in my life. I am thankful to God for the strength He gives me from day to day. Giving up is never an option. With God on my side, I know I will be alright.

By writing this book, I am aware that I may lose some people, but this is not about them; it is about me and the things I need to do to make my life better. It is time to remove the mask and be **FREE**! I am now ready to help other women overcome the things I went through because I can speak to that space. God prepared me for everything I have and will go through in my life. Had I not endured, how would I be able to help another woman be freed from abuse, neglect, homelessness, pain, criminal cases, parenting, and HIV/AIDS? Often, we do not understand why we go through different things in life. Sometimes, we go through for others and not for ourselves.

Some women are afraid to share their real and raw story, and that is okay. When it is their time, they will tell it. I just pray it will not be too late to help others.

I never knew the depths of my strength until my HIV diagnosis in 2015. At the time, I thought it was going to be the end of the world for me. Instead, I used it as fuel to propel me to be greater. After all, if God did not think I could handle it, I would not have it. I will not sit around feeling sorry for myself.

I pray that God sends me a man who will accept me for who I am and will love me through my brokenness. I pray that man will embrace and support me. I pray he will be there when I need encouragement and wipe away my tears when I do not have a good day. I pray my God-given man will encourage me to keep going when I have no fight left in me. I pray he will be by my side when it feels as if there is no one else left in the world. I pray he will be my laughter when I am filled with sadness and assure me that I am the only woman in his world.

Pray *specific* prayers, ladies.

I know no man is perfect. I have endured my fair share of heartache and pain at the hands of men since the age of fifteen. I do, however, know I deserve the same level of love I give. I deserve happiness. My prayer is that I will not be judged by my past but instead accepted in my present from this day forth.

This Lovely Butterfly needs all the prayers and support she can get — something I say unashamedly.

To my play sisters, Pastor and First Lady, and the friends whom God has given me who have played their part in my journey and encouraged me to keep on keeping on:

I am thankful for you ALL and promise to keep living MY blessed and favored life!

About the Author

Darlene Kearney was born in Dallas, Texas, and raised in Houston, Texas, in the projects named Aristocrats Apartments. She has a successful educational venture, including attending Hobby Elementary, Dick Dowling Middle School, Stephen F. Austin High School, and the Contemporary Learning Center. She earned an Associate's Degree in Mental Health Services-Mental Health Clinical and Counseling Psychology. Darlene is presently attending University of Houston-Downtown in pursuit of her Bachelor's in Social Work.

Darlene loves giving back to the community. You can reach her via email at godslovelybutterflies@gmail.com.